CAPTAIN THOMAS MACDONOUGH

DELAWARE BORN HERO
OF THE BATTLE
OF LAKE CHAMPLAIN

Virginia M. Burdick

Delaware Heritage Press
Wilmington, Delaware

Captain Thomas Macdonough
Delaware Born Hero of the Battle of Lake Champlain

by Virginia M. Burdick

A DELAWARE HERITAGE PRESS BOOK

First Printing, September 1991

ISBN: 0-924117-04-4

Library of Congress Catalog Card Number: 91-73590

The Delaware Heritage Commission
Carvel State Office Building
820 North French Street, 4th Floor
Wilmington, Delaware 19801

Many Thanks to Many Friends

During Plattsburgh's celebration in 1989 of the 175th anniversary of the Battle of Lake Champlain, I talked with my eleven-year-old grandson, Daniel, about the victory. His interest in the hero gave me the idea to write a story about Thomas Macdonough. Several months later Daniel read my manuscript and made this comment, "I like the story, Nana, but I think you should explain better how the ships were turned around." I followed my grandson's advice and wrote a more detailed account of Macdonough's life. Without the support of the Delaware Heritage Commission and loyal friends, this story would not have been published.

Rodney McDonough and Isabelle McDonough Verkaart encouraged me to write about their great-grandfather, Captain Thomas Macdonough. My college roommate, Grace L. Davis, was enthusiastic about the short story I wrote for the seventh grade pupils. Dr. Allan S. Everest, local authority on the War of 1812, explained historical facts and proofread my manuscript. Helen Allan, director of Clinton County Historical Museum, lent me negatives of pictures pertaining to the naval and land battles. Jeffrey Kelley, director of the Kent-Delord House Museum gave me copies of the letters of Macdonough and Henry Delord. Richard Ward assisted me by researching old newspapers on microfilm. Glyndon Cole, director of Special Collections at the Plattsburgh Public Library, helped me find Macdonough information.

My husband, Charles, a retired English teacher, patiently corrected my spelling, grammar and punctuation.

Despite sleet, snowbanks and ice storms, Susan Seguin drove in daily from the country to type my manuscript. Barbara McEwing from the Historical Society of Delaware and members of the Delaware Heritage Commission in Wilmington sent me information I could not find here.

I was pleased to receive, March 14, 1991, permission from the publisher, Syracuse University Press, to use material in Allan Everest's book, *The War of 1812 in the Champlain Valley* (Syracuse: Syracuse University Press, 1981).

Virginia M. Burdick
Plattsburgh, New York
March, 1991

The Delaware Heritage Commission wishes to acknowledge the cooperation and services of a number of persons and agencies. The agencies which cooperated in the collection and sharing of data are the Historical Society of Delaware, the State of Delaware Archives in Dover, the Hagley Library. The Departments of Correction and Transportation cleared the family cemetery.

Professional persons who have added to this book are Adriana Daniels with her contemporary photographs and Mary Beth Heaney with her graphics. Jean and Howard Row of the Commission edited an early version.

Brigitta Moulson, the current owner of the home, opened her doors on a number of occasions for our inspection and questions. And, without the postcard collection of William E. Dill, we would not have several of the nice illustrations to include.

Contents

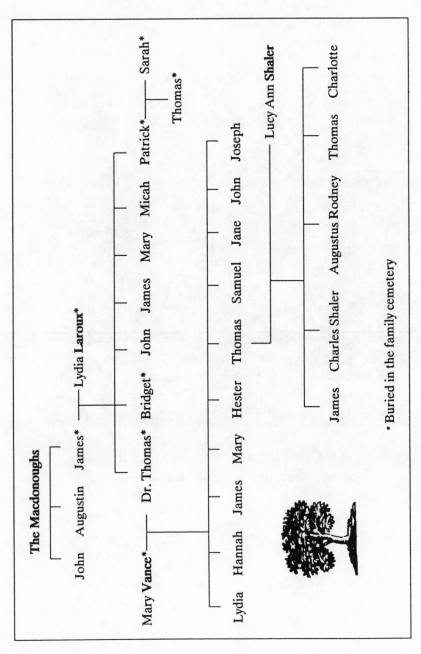

The Family of Thomas Macdonough

Late 19th century postcard view of
Macdonough family homestead

Chapter I
Boyhood at the Trap

This story about Captain Thomas Macdonough begins with James McDonough, his grandfather. James migrated from Ireland to Delaware in 1725 and settled at the Trap, St. Georges Hundred, New Castle County, Delaware. The name Trap refers to McDonough's farm and also to a nearby settlement about six miles from Middletown. The Trap village was named McDonough in 1844 by the post office. James was a physician and a man of strong character. James had two brothers. John settled in Newtown, Long Island, and Augustin went to the East Indies.

In 1746 James married Lydia Laroux, also of St. Georges Hundred. They had seven children: Thomas, Bridget, John, James, Patrick, Mary, and Micah.

Their oldest son, Thomas, studied medicine and became a physician. In 1770 he married Mary Vance, a neighbor of the McDonoughs.

In March 1776 Delaware elected Dr. McDonough to be a major in a battalion in the Revolutionary War. Major McDonough immediately joined the command at Dover, Delaware. He was a commander at the battle of Long Island in August, where he won the praise of General George Washington for gallantry, and in the battle of White Plains, New York, October 28. Here he received a wound which incapacitated him from active duty the last two months of service. The battalion was disbanded in

January 1777 and the major received an honorable discharge.

During the remainder of his life Dr. Thomas served his state in many civic positions. During his service on the Privy Council[1] he became a "close friend of Caesar Rodney,"[2] who was elected president of Delaware March 31, 1778. Caesar Rodney's nephew, Caesar Augustus Rodney, was also a friend of Dr. Thomas and his son, Captain Thomas.

In 1788 Dr. McDonough was elected third Justice of the Court of Common Pleas and Orphans Court of New Castle County. In 1791 he was elected second Justice of these courts.

The records of St. Ann's Episcopal Church at Middletown show that Major McDonough was one of the wardens in 1793 and 1794.

During the early years of their marriage, Dr. Thomas and Mary McDonough lived in a small log house at the Trap. Here, on December 31, 1783, was born Thomas, Jr., their sixth child and second son, who would be a navy hero.

The following year, 1784, the family moved to a large brick house built on land owned by James McDonough, father of Dr. Thomas and grandfather of Thomas, Jr. Here four more McDonoughs came into the family. Young Thomas's brothers and sisters were: Lydia, Hannah, James, Mary, Hester, Samuel, Jane, John, and Joseph.

During these times the main house consisted of only one principal room downstairs and two smaller rooms on the second floor. However, the use of brick and the fine interior woodwork as displayed in the fully panelled end wall on the second floor indicate that, despite the apparent

10

smallness of the dwelling, its builder and residents were people of superior affluence in the immediate area of St. Georges Hundred. This is further borne out by Patrick MacDonough's 1803 inventory which listed among other things six yellow Windsor chairs, an eight-day clock, silver items such as teaspoons, sugar tongs and a creamer, and a "pleasure sleigh." Other buildings at this time were a granary, corn crib, smokehouse, and kitchen.[3]

The McDonough children had a happy childhood on their father's farm and often visited their grandparents nearby. According to the stories of their neighbors, the McDonough boys liked to play jokes on the residents of the Trap village.

A legend told by Lewis Vandegrift in Volume XVII of the papers on the Historical Society of Delaware recalls this tendency of the McDonough boys. It seems that brother James ordered a coffin for a certain lady he assured the coffin-maker "was on the brink of death." The tradesman worked through the night but, on delivery of the coffin, lo and behold he saw the lady walking out her front door. He was so angry, he insisted that James pay for the coffin. James, with the assistance of his laughing brothers, took the burial piece home and propped it up in a corner. And there it stood for years, Vandegrift says, "a receptacle for good cheer and hospitality."[4]

In 1822, Captain Macdonough wrote from Middletown, Connecticut to his sister Lydia in Delaware:

I should like to visit the old home where I have spent some youthful, happy hours; to stroll about the fields and woods as I used to do.[5]

11

Thomas	Patrick	Sarah McNunn
died	died	died
Dec. 23, 1817	Sep. 27, 1803	March 26, 1827

Macdonough family graveyard

In his moments of nostalgia Macdonough's thoughts probably turned back to happy winter evenings with his family gathered around the fireplace at the Trap farm. The children listened spellbound to their father's stories of the hardships and courage of Revolutionary War soldiers.

Macdonough's parents did not live to an old age. His mother, Mary, died in 1792 at the age of 41. Three years later Dr. Thomas died at age 48. The commodore's parents were buried beside his grandparents, James and Lydia, in a small plot near the Macdonough homestead at the Trap.

Thomas, Jr. was twelve years old when his father died. No doubt his uncle Patrick helped Thomas's oldest sister, Lydia, care for the orphaned children still at home. With the next generation, Thomas, Jr. changed the spelling of his name to Macdonough.

The reader will notice throughout the book that Thomas's last name will be spelled in two ways, depending on the historical work quoted from. The McDonoughs and the Macdonoughs are the same family.

Another small confusion in this story is the reference to the Middletowns. As a boy Thomas lived near Middletown, Delaware, and when he married he lived in Middletown, Connecticut.

Finally, we refer to Thomas Macdonough as "the Commodore." This term was given him after the battle on Lake Champlain but it was not an official rank used by the navy in those days. He was Captain Macdonough. It is more an affectionate and honorary title than real.

Ships Thomas Macdonough Sailed

Ship	Date		Purpose
Ganges	May 15	1800	War with France
Constellation	October 20	1801	To cruise in Mediterranean
Constellation	July	1802	Fought in Tripoli
Philadelphia	August	1803	Tripoli
Enterprise	December 14	1803	To rescue the *Philadelphia*
Intrepid	February 16	1804	To burn the *Philadelphia*
Enterprise	June 3	1805	Peace with Tripoli
Syren		1806	
	Summer	1806	Went for visit to Middletown, Connecticut
Wasp	January	1807	
	March	1807	Recruiting
Gulliver	March	1809	Commercial ship (Traveled to East India for one year)
	August	1811	(back in charge of gunboats)
Jeannette Snow	March 12	1812	Commercial ship
	June	1812	War with Great Britain

14

Chapter II
Sailor in Training

After a few years as a teenage clerk in a store in Middletown, Delaware, Macdonough decided to ask for an appointment to the United States Navy. His brother, James, was a midshipman (sailor in training) and probably told Thomas exciting stories of the hardships and glory of life at sea. The accounts of the patriotism of his father and two uncles during the Revolution also influenced Macdonough.

With the help of a senator from Delaware, Macdonough's request was granted. The first sentence he wrote in the journal he was required to keep announced his acceptance into the Navy:

> On the 5th of February, 1800, I received a warrant as midshipman in the navy (I was then 16 years old) of the United States from John Adams, then President, through the influence of Mr. Latimer, a senator from the state of Delaware.[6]

After his appointment, Macdonough was ordered to the U.S. ship *Ganges,* a 24-gun corvette (a smaller edition of the frigate) on May 15, 1800, and remained on her for a year. From New Castle, Delaware, the *Ganges* sailed to the West Indies, where the United States was at war with France. The *Ganges* crew captured three French ships and sent them to the United States. All the armed ships of this period had guns only along the one upper deck. They were also powered by the wind and sails propelled them forward. So on calm days they didn't move very far.

While they were at sea, yellow fever broke out on board the *Ganges*, and many sailors and officers died. Macdonough fell victim to the disease and, with other midshipmen, was taken to Havana and "put into a dirty Spanish hospital."[7] He recovered and after many difficulties finally arrived home. Thomas described those final hours of his journey home.

Took passage on board the ferry boat, crossed the Chesapeake Bay and, travelling up through the country, got out of the stage at the Trap, my native place, after an absence of nearly a year, with straw hat, canvas shoes and in other respects poor enough.[8]

Macdonough's relatives and friends were surprised that he had survived the yellow fever epidemic–in fact some had thought he was dead.

Life was not easy for these young sailors. Midshipman Macdonough was paid $19.00 a month and allowed one ration a day. A typical Saturday's ration was a pound of pork, half a pound of peas or beans, four ounces of cheese. Every day he received a pound of bread with half a pint of distilled spirits or a quart of beer. Discipline was so strict that "only the most rugged and determined could remain in the service for any length of time."[9] For a full dress uniform Macdonough wore a:

Gilbert Stuart Portrait of Lt. Thomas Macdonough

coat of blue cloth with short lapels faced with same and ornamented with six buttons, standing collar with a diamond formed of gold lace on each side not exceeding two inches square, slashed sleeves with small buttons, all the button holes worked with gold thread; single breasted blue vest with flaps, no buttons to the pockets, blue or white breeches; gold laced cocked hat, shoes with buckles and a hanger. ... Dirks were not to be worn on shore.[10]

About this time, April 30, 1798, to be exact, the Department of the Navy was created. Up until then it had been part of the office of the Secretary of War. In preparation for this event, and since a young navy needed ships, three American ships had been commissioned in 1794: the *Constitution,* the *Constellation* and the *United States.* The first one finished was the *Constellation,* nicknamed the *Yankee Racehorse.* It had a crew of 368. It was not as heavy as the *Constitution,* and it had 36 guns. (The *Constitution* had 44.) The ship was built of various woods—live oak, white oak, yellow pine and Douglas fir. (The *Constellation* is now in the Baltimore, Maryland, harbor, where it may be boarded by visitors.)

Both Thomas and James served as midshipmen on the *Constellation* , but in different years. James was on board the *Constellation* in 1799 when it made its first conquest. He had helped to win the war against the French although its toll for him was great—the loss of a leg and the need to leave the navy for good.

The story goes like this. James was a midshipman under Truxton's command on the *Constellation* when it captured the (French ship) *Insurgente* in the West Indies. James was wounded by a musket ball in the ankle so severely that his leg was amputated. James was very brave . . . when he spoke with his men in the hospital after his wounding, he said he could distinctly perceive the enemy aiming and firing at him.[11]

After the ratification of the peace treaty with France on February 3, 1801, Congress authorized President Thomas Jefferson to sell most of the vessels belonging to the navy. Many seamen and early officers lost their jobs. Thomas Macdonough wrote in his journal that through the influence of Caesar Augustus Rodney, "my father's and my friend,"[12] he was not dismissed.

At the end of this war with France, the United States Navy was only three years old.

On October 20, 1801, Thomas was ordered to join the *Constellation* for its cruise in the Mediterranean sea. The following July the *Constellation* fought Tripolitanian gunboats at Tripoli. Macdonough noted in his journal that guns from the Tripoli fort threw their shot over his ship. The young United States found itself at war with Tripoli over that country's demands for payment to leave American ships unharmed.

In 1803 Congress ordered the construction of more ships for our war with Tripoli. Macdonough's furlough with his family was shortened when he was ordered to join the *Philadelphia*, a 38-gun frigate. His ship arrived at Gibraltar in August. In October a ship from Tripoli captured the *Philadelphia* and took it to Tripoli. It was Macdonough's good fortune that he was absent from his ship when the *Philadelphia* and her crew were taken.

However he was not to be parted from the *Philadelphia* for long.

On December 14 Macdonough was ordered to the *Enterprise*. The *Enterprise* was a somewhat different ship design. It was a 12-gun schooner. It was thought schooners would be able to maneuver faster than the frigates. Here he became a close friend of the ship's commander, Lieutenant Stephen Decatur. They were both in their early twenties, active, daring and dedicated to their work.

The 17th of December 1803 Commodore Preble of the *Constitution* and Decatur and Macdonough on the *Enterprise* sailed to Tripoli with plans to rescue the *Philadelphia*. However, they decided it would be too hazardous to board the ship in the harbor. Instead they would try to destroy her to prevent the enemy from using the *Philadelphia*.

On February 16, 1804, Decatur's volunteers from the *Enterprise* sailed into Tripoli Bay on the *Intrepid*, a small boat. Each man was given the order to burn a specific part of the *Philadelphia*. Macdonough and ten men were to set fire to the berth deck and forward storeroom. The *Philadelphia* was moored "in the inner harbor ... and within easy range . . . of the batteries of the harbor. She mounted 40 guns . . . a full complement of men was on board to serve them."[13] The *Intrepid*'s men must have known they were facing death or imprisonment if their plans failed. With a light breeze and the shadows of evening, the *Intrepid* slowly approached the inner harbor.

The following portions of Decatur's report to Commodore Preble give a vivid description of the burning of the *Philadelphia:*

The stranding and capture of the *Philadelphia*
Etching by Joseph F. Sabin

Stealthily she (the *Intrepid*) slunk along in the gloom with all but a few of her crew concealed.... Unchallenged by guard boat or sentry she crept by the forts and had drawn quite close to the *Philadelphia* when the (enemy's) frigate hailed her ... the *Intrepid*'s pilot replied that the ship was a trader from Malta, that she had lost her anchors in the recent storm and that they desired permission to make fast to the frigate during the night. It was then about half past nine o'clock. Meanwhile a boat's crew from the *Intrepid* attached a line to the *Philadelphia*'s forechain. ... Hauling on these lines the crew, still concealed, had brought their vessels almost alongside when the Turks were aroused; the cry 'Americanos' rang through the ship... [14]

A moment later the *Intrepid*'s crew boarded the *Philadelphia* and set her on fire. In twenty-five minutes the frigate was in flames. With difficulty the *Intrepid* moved away from the burning ship and out from the harbor. They had succeeded in their mission to destroy the *Philadelphia* so that the enemy could not claim it as its own. According to Frank Bowen writing about this instance, "It was one of the most gallant cutting-out expeditions in history, and the total loss on the American side was only one man wounded."[15] However, dangerous and exciting adventures seemed to happen quite often to young Thomas. On another occasion, while Macdonough was on the *Enterprise* he had a confrontation with bandits at Messina on the island of Sicily. Some reports say the incident occurred at Syracuse. According to the *Analectic Magazine* of March 1816,

22

Macdonough remained on shore one night later than usual.

He hired a boat to take him back to the schooner. When he saw the boat was manned by three men instead of two, the usual complement, he became suspicious and refused to get into her. Thereupon the three men attacked him with their daggers. Macdonough defended himself with his sword and succeeded in wounding two of his assailants. The third took flight, pursued by Thomas, his intended victim. Running into a building, the assailant mounted to the roof, and then, finding all other means of escape impossible, jumped to the ground, but was killed by the fall.[16]

Perhaps the winter of 1805 was a little quieter. Macdonough spent these months in Venice, where the *Enterprise* was hauled up for repairs. From there he went to Ancona to prepare gunboats for Tripoli. When Macdonough arrived in Syracuse with his squadron, peace had been declared between Tripoli and the United States, June 3, 1805.

Macdonough wrote in his journal that he "remained in the squadron during all its operations against Tripoli, presented the flags of the captured boats to Commodore Preble . . . and was in 1805 or 1806 appointed by the Commodore a lieutenant of the *Enterprise*."[17] He called these years in the Mediterranean "the school where our navy received its first lessons."[18]

23

During his free time Macdonough visited Naples, Rome, Pompeii and the towns of Barbary Powers. Thereafter he returned to the United States, where he remained some two or three years.

During these years British sailors preferred to work on American merchant ships where they would have better treatment and wages. When the British authorities boarded American merchant ships hunting for British deserters, they often kidnapped American seamen. This act of capturing, or impressing, our sailors was known as impressment. The United States had tried to stop this cruel and illegal act, but Great Britain continued to impress our sailors.

Macdonough himself was so captured. The story goes that Thomas Macdonough was impressed by the English in Liverpool and put on one of their ships. He was assigned to sleeping quarters with a corporal of the guard. Macdonough waited until the corporal was sound asleep. Then he stole the corporal's clothes, put them on and went up to the spar deck. It was a dark night so he stood in the shadows while inquiring of the sentry regarding identification of a boat anchored at the boom. "I think there is rum aboard her, sir" he said. "Very well ... search her" was the sentry's reply. At that moment Macdonough saw the head of the corporal whose clothes he had stolen appearing in the hatchway. Macdonough immediately knocked him down, jumped into the boat, broke it loose and was on his way. The sentry discharged his muskets but Macdonough safely made shore and swore, "If I live, I'll make England remember the day she impressed an American soldier." ... And he did![19]

Then Macdonough personally rescued an American sailor in 1806 from a British ship. He wrote in his journal:

> When I was first lieutenant of the *Syren* brig (a 16 gun schooner), an occurrence took place in the harbor of Gibraltar which excited a good deal of feeling both on the side of the English and ourselves. A British man-of-war's boat boarded an American merchantman which lay near the *Syren* and took out, or impressed, one of her men. I went alongside the British boat in one of ours and demanded him, which demand was refused. I then took hold of the man and took him in my boat and brought him on board the *Syren*. He was an American and of course we kept him.[20]

Six years later Macdonough would help his country defeat Great Britain and end the impressment of our seamen. Author Rodney Macdonough was justly proud of his grandfather when he summed up Thomas Macdonough's training in the Mediterranean Sea:

> They were years of . . . hard work, plenty of danger and excitement, some pleasure and not a little personal distinction. His service in the Mediterranean . . . was the best training a young officer could have had. . . . He acquired the habits of self-reliance and self-restraint. Naturally impetuous, he was taught to temper rashness with discretion. He learned that obedience to his superiors was the best way to compel obedience to himself. . . [21]

Types of Ships Macdonough Sailed

Sloop A sloop is a single-masted sailing vessel with a mainsail, a jib and sometimes other sails. The *Wasp* was an 18-gun sloop.

Brig The *Gulliver* was a brig, which is a two-masted, square-rigged ship.

Schooner A fore and aft rigged vessel with two or more masts. Both the 12-gun *Enterprise* and the 16 -gun *Syren* were schooners.

Frigate The largest of the ships, the frigate is a fast sailing, three-masted sailing warship moved by oars or sails. The *Essex* (32-guns), *Philadelphia* (38-guns) and *Constellation* (44 guns) were frigates.

While on leave the summer of 1806 Macdonough went to the Trap to visit his brothers and sisters. He had been away from his home for three years. His family must have been spellbound when Macdonough described the burning of the *Philadelphia* and his rescue of the American sailor on the British ship.

In October Macdonough was ordered to Middletown, Connecticut, to work under Captain Isaac Hull superintending the construction of gunboats. During his three months there he became acquainted with the family of Nathaniel Shaler. His lovely and gracious daughter, Lucy Ann, was 16 years old. The lieutenant was 23 years old. They would wait six more years before they could be married.

In January of 1807 Macdonough went to Washington to join the *Wasp*, an 18-gun sloop of war (a sloop is a single masted sailing ship with one headsail). At that time the Senate confirmed his nomination as lieutenant. In March he was in New York to enlist men for the ship. While there he wrote his friend, William Vandeursen of Middletown, Connecticut, on March 11, 1807:

Dear Van,
Pardon me, my good fellow, for not writing you sooner, but I assure you I have been so busy shipping men for the ship and so many damn things in the way that I have no time. I did not get your letter till a few days ago, when I arrived in Washington. I came on here to ship the remainder of the crew (one hundred men) and expect to be at least a month in shipping

them owing to the low wages. In the meantime you must write me often for the ship is ready for sea and will sail immediately the above men are procured. . . . I would make this longer but the sailors are making such a noise together with the Drum and Fife they confuse me or would the Devil himself, who has a larger rendezvous open than I have. . . .[22]

Macdonough was ordered to join the frigate *Essex* in March, 1809, as first lieutenant. The speed of a frigate was very slow compared with the ships of today. The maximum speed was 12 knots. . . The average time of a westward passage from New York to London was 38 days (compared with 5-7 nowadays). He remained on the *Essex* until September, when he was directed to take charge of the gunboats in Connecticut and Long Island.

In spite of Macdonough being ordered from ship to ship to prepare for the ultimate battle on Lake Champlain, he seemed to have been liked by the regular sailors. Evidence of Macdonough's fairness and popularity are contained in the following letter which he received when he was transferred from the *Essex*:

Sep. 6th 1809

Respected Sir;
We . . . learn with heartfelt sorrow your intention of leaving the Ship. Permit us, Sir, . . . to return you our most Sincere thanks for your officer-like Conduct and Philanthropy during the time we have had the happiness of being under your command as Second officer. We don't wish to trouble you with a great

Harangue. We can only assure you, Sir, that we all feel as one in the cause of regret at your about to leave the Ship. We do Sincerely Wish and hope your Successor will tread the steps which you have to Render the Crew as Comfortable as possible. . . We wish you all the happiness that man can enjoy, and may He who holds the Destiny of Man guide you Safe through life and Pilot you at last to the Harbour of Rest is the Hearty prayer of the Subscribers.[23]

While Macdonough had charge of gunboats in Middletown, Connecticut, in 1809, he enjoyed the friendship of Lucy Ann and her family. But his job was boring and not very lucrative. There was little chance of advancement for a young lieutenant planning to be married. He wrote in his journal that the "navy was unpopular and many officers quitted it."[24]

Although Macdonough was tempted to resign from the navy, he decided instead to ask for a furlough to join the merchant service. Such a leave of absence was common for American naval officers at that time. The Navy Department granted him permission to make a commercial East India voyage in the spring of 1810. In June he left New York in command of the *Gulliver*, a brig. (Brigs carry square sails so they can move faster before the wind.) The next year he returned safely with a large cargo which was sold at auction in Boston.

As soon as Macdonough was free of the *Gulliver* he returned to Middletown. On August 25, 1811, he sent a report to the Secretary of the Navy, Paul Hamilton, in

Washington. He informed Hamilton he had already promised to take another ship to India and presumed the navy would give him permission. Hamilton promptly answered he would not give Macdonough a furlough. Although Macdonough was reluctant to leave the navy, he probably needed the money that a second commercial voyage would provide him. And life for him in the navy at that moment must have been a waiting game. So on September 26 he wrote Hamilton he would like his permission to resign. He got no immediate answer. So he wrote again that he was waiting for an answer. At that point the Secretary of the Navy had had enough correspondence with Lt. Thomas Macdonough. Hamilton kept Macdonough's last letter and on it wrote: "Resignation to be accepted. P.H."[25] Luckily for America, at a later date someone crossed out these four words.

On his second merchant voyage, Macdonough left New York March 12, 1812, for Lisbon in command of the *Jeannette Snow*. He had a quarter interest in the ship and her cargo. However, the voyage was interrupted by a nonintercourse law passed by Congress on April 4, 1812. It put an embargo of ninety days on American trade with foreign countries. For several years Congress had enforced these retaliatory acts to stop British harassment of our ships, the impressment of our seamen and interference with Indians in the Northwest Territory.

When it became apparent that these measures could no longer avert war, President James Madison sent a war message to Congress June 1. War with Great Britain was declared June 18, 1812.

It was the end of commercial ship work for Macdonough. He left the *Jeannette Snow*, and returned to Middletown, Connecticut. He became even better acquainted with Lucy Ann Shaler and her family and joined the Episcopal Church. Although his own parents attended St. Ann's Episcopal Church in Middletown, Delaware, Macdonough was not confirmed as a member before he left home.

When war against England was declared, it took nearly a week for the news to reach Macdonough. Of course he immediately wrote to the Secretary of the Navy Hamilton.

Middletown, June 26th 1812

Sir: The United States now being at war, I solicit your order for service in the navy and hope you will favor me with such a situation as in your opinion I am suited to hold.

I have the honor to be, sir, your most obt. (obedient) sert. (servant)

T. Macdonough[26]

In August Macdonough once again received an order to command a division of gunboats, this time in Portland, Maine. He arrived there September 7 and left a month later, having received an exciting new assignment. In his journal Macdonough made this entry:

After remaining a few months at Portland I was ordered by Mr. Madison to take command of the vessels on Lake Champlain. Proceeded thither across the country through the Notch of the White

32

Mountains, partly on horseback, carrying my bundle with a valise on behind and a country lad only in company to return with my horses. I arrived fatigued at Burlington (Vermont) on the lake in about four days and took command of the vessels after waiting on the commanding general, Bloomfield.[27]

It is not surprising that Macdonough was tired when he reached his destination. A sailor is not accustomed to being jolted in a carriage and on horseback for mile after mile. His papers include a bill for $75 for the use of "a horse and chaise."[28]

Macdonough's journal does not reveal his reaction to the new orders. We can only surmise that the young lieutenant was elated and probably eager to shoulder the momentous responsibility of defeating the British.

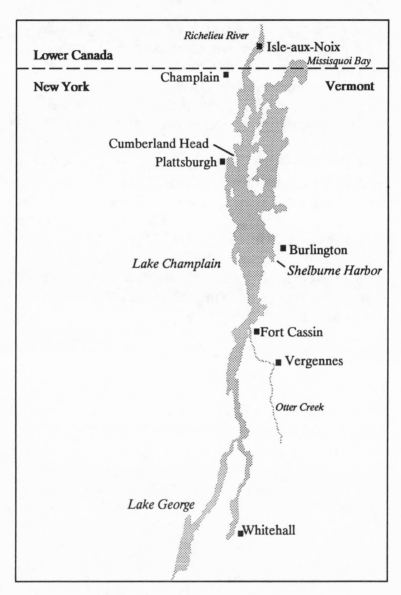

Champlain Valley 1812-1814

Chapter III
Hero of Lake Champlain

As Macdonough rode over rutted, winding, dirt roads through the White Mountains of New Hampshire and the Green Mountains of Vermont, he had four days to appreciate the brilliant autumn foliage. Most of the time the lieutenant was probably engrossed in plans for his new command on Lake Champlain. After twelve years of training on oceans and seas in a mild climate, he would have to adjust to a small lake and cold weather. Naturally Macdonough's plans included his beloved Lucy Ann. With a monthly salary of $50, he could support Lieutenant and Mrs. Thomas Macdonough.

The day he arrived in Burlington, Vermont, Macdonough walked along the village's shore on Lake Champlain. Looking west across the lake he could see the lofty Adirondack Mountains rising up from the New York State shore. Here the lake is twelve miles wide, the widest part of the lake. It stretches approximately 130 miles from the southern end at Whitehall, New York, north to the boundary of the United States and British Canada.

Macdonough's first official duty was to meet with General Henry Dearborn in command of both the army and navy at Plattsburgh, New York. He needed to gather information about preparations for the war. Most importantly, he must tactfully and firmly inform the elderly general that he, Lt. Thomas Macdonough, was now in command of the navy by order from President Madison.

When Macdonough's boat sailed into Plattsburgh's harbor, probably on October 9, 1812, he had his first view of the twenty-seven-year-old village. It was situated at the mouth of the Saranac River and had about 300 inhabitants. There were seventy-eight houses, four hotels, thirteen stores, mills, a blockhouse, courthouse and jail. A school and a church were under construction.[29]

By the time Macdonough called on Dearborn, the general had received orders from the War Department to give Lt. Macdonough six sloops (vessels with one mast). They were used to transport troops on the Lake Champlain frontier. No doubt Macdonough showed Dearborn the order of September 28 which he received from the Navy Department:

> Six vessels have been purchased by the War Department and there are two gunboats built by the navy on the lake, the whole of which is to be under your direction and command.[30]

Dearborn strongly opposed the separation of the navy and army departments. Reluctantly he gave Macdonough five sloops and kept the *President*, the largest and best sloop. Macdonough took the *Hunter* and the *Bull Dog*, but left the others. When Macdonough went to Basin Harbor, south of Burlington, to take charge of the navy's gunboats, he discovered the former navy commander, Sidney Smith, had left the boats on the beach. "One was partly sunk and the seams of both were so open as almost to admit the hand."[31] We can imagine his reaction when he saw the navy's derelict gunboats.

36

On October 13, 1812, Macdonough sailed with his sloops and gunboats south to the shipyards of Whitehall. He immediately hired carpenters to prepare his vessels for war. In a letter to Captain Isaac Hull in New York, he asked for naval supplies and sailors. The equipment finally reached Albany on Hudson River boats. But it took several days for teams of horses to haul heavy loads seventy-eight miles over bad roads from Albany to Whitehall. Macdonough's problem of securing a crew was never solved. The men disliked working in severe winter weather far from populated areas. He was impatient with the local carpenters, who knew nothing about warships.

After two weeks of hard work with the men, Macdonough was ready to take his converted, patched-up warships down the lake to Plattsburgh.[32] The *Hunter*, with Lt. Sidney Smith, carried two twelve-pound guns and one long eighteen-pounder on a pivot. The *Bull Dog*, with Macdonough, was armed with six-pounders and a long eighteen-pounder on a pivot. Eventually Dearborn turned the *President* over to Macdonough. It became his flagship after it was armed with eight guns.

The last of October, 1812, Macdonough took his little fleet to Plattsburgh to patrol the lake. When cold weather arrived in early December, he put his vessels in winter quarters at Shelburne Harbor, south of Burlington. In his journal Macdonough describes the vessels as his "poor forlorn-looking squadron."[33] This is one of the few times that Macdonough's journal reflects his emotions.

Early in December the Navy Department gave Macdonough permission to go to Middletown, Connecticut. His assignment was to marry the young lady who had waited six years to be his wife. Lt. Thomas Macdonough and Miss Lucy Ann Shaler were married at Middletown's Episcopal Church December 12, 1812. Macdonough stood waiting at the altar in his full dress uniform, blue coat trimmed with gold lace, a gold epaulet on his right shoulder. His sword hung from his black belt. He held his gold-laced cocked hat in his left hand.[34] According to the *Middlesex Gazette*, Lucy Ann wore a long silk damask dress of hyacinth color. Her head dress was shaped like a bonnet. The bride was twenty-two years old. The bridegroom was twenty-eight years old.

Lieutenant and Mrs. Thomas Macdonough took a week with horse and chaise to drive to Vermont. On December 19 they arrived at Tousey's Tavern in Burlington.[35]

After Macdonough checked the vessels at their winter quarters, he took Lucy Ann for a sleigh ride twenty miles down the frozen lake to Plattsburgh. He wanted his bride to have a social visit there while he called on Peter Sailly, Collector of Customs in the Champlain District. For four years Sailly had tried to enforce the laws against smuggling between the United States and British Canada. Residents of northern Vermont and New York hated the embargo acts which prevented a lucrative trade with their neighbors across the Canadian border. Sailly needed the navy's gunboats to guard the border. Macdonough needed information about the British navy that Sailly and an Indian spy could send him.

It was doubtless at the Sailly home that Thomas and Lucy Ann met Henry and Betsey Delord. They were

Home of the Delords: Plattsburgh, New York
Friends of Macdonough

neighbors and close friends of the Saillys. The Delords became fond of the Macdonoughs and entertained them frequently. When the young couple sat at Betsey's tea table in the Delords' east parlor, they could see the lake where the American navy would meet the British. The Delord homestead, now a museum, still stands on the north bank of the Saranac River.

The summer of 1813 was a disaster for Macdonough and his little fleet. On June 2 Macdonough ordered Lt. Sidney Smith with the sloop *Growler* and Sailing Master Loomis with the *Eagle* to sail north to the Canadian border. They were to block the mouth of the Richelieu River to prevent British ships from entering Lake Champlain. They had specific orders not to sail beyond the line where the lake becomes the Richelieu River. Lt. Smith deliberately sailed into British territory. After a battle of four hours the enemy captured our sloops and sent the men to prison. With our repaired sloops added to their fleet, the British now had control of Lake Champlain.

In his journal Macdonough mildly refers to the "imprudence of Lt. Sidney Smith."[36] When he received the news of Smith's disobedience, Macdonough must have been outraged and discouraged.

Macdonough on June 4, 1813, sent a report of the loss to the new Secretary of the Navy, William Jones. On the 17th, Secretary Jones sent Macdonough the following orders:

> ... regain by every possible exertion the ascendancy which we have lost, for which purpose you are authorized to purchase, arm and equip ... two of the

40

best sloops . . . to be procured on the lake. . . . You have unlimited authority to procure the necessary resources of men, material and munitions for that purpose. I rely upon your efficient and prudent use of the authority vested in you. . . . The naval command is exclusively vested in you and for which you are held responsible.[37]

Encouraged by William Jones's confidence in him, Macdonough immediately made plans to rebuild his squadron.

On July 24, 1813, Lt. Thomas Macdonough was designated master commandant. He was called "commodore" out of respect or courtesy even though that rank did not exist at that time.

The last of July a British flotilla under Colonel John Murray landed at Plattsburgh's wharf. Murray promised the frightened citizens that his men would not destroy private property. The militia was called out, but promptly fled when they saw about 1,000 soldiers burning public buildings and stealing the contents of private homes. Families packed up and fled south to a Quaker settlement in Peru, New York. The Delords buried their silver tea set in their garden before Betsey joined her friends in Peru, ten miles south of Plattsburgh.

In August some of the British vessels sailed to Burlington to attack the fleet that Macdonough's carpenters were repairing. After the British and Americans exchanged gunfire, the enemy sailed south to raid more villages. Macdonough did not meet the British on the broad lake because his vessels were not sufficiently repaired.

41

By the middle of August Macdonough's boats were ready, but not his manpower. Finally with soldiers borrowed from the army at Plattsburgh, Macdonough sailed out on Lake Champlain September 6. He could now control the lake.

In December, 1813, Macdonough put his fleet in winter quarters at Vergennes, Vermont, a small village twenty miles south of Burlington. His vessels were located on Otter Creek seven miles from its mouth at Lake Champlain. At the foot of the falls Macdonough built a shipyard. Nearby were forges, mills, iron works, and plenty of trees. The village had a tavern, stores and hospitable families. Macdonough did not worry about the enemy's invasion. The river was deep, but so narrow and crooked there was little chance of an attack.

Secretary of the Navy Jones on January 28, 1814, authorized Macdonough to build gunboats or a ship. The lieutenant chose to build a large ship. The brothers Adam and Noah Brown from New York promised to construct a ship in sixty days. To everyone's surprise and delight the Browns completed their work in forty days.

On April 11 Lucy Ann Macdonough christened the ship. Like the schooner which engaged the brig Rachel in 1812, it too was named the *Saratoga* to commemorate our country's victory at Saratoga, New York, during the Revolution. The ship lacked naval equipment. Roads from Troy and Boston were impassable. "It took eighty teams of horses to carry one consignment of naval stores from Troy to Vergennes and then three large cables were left behind."[38]

The schooner *Saratoga* captures the brig *Rachel*
December 15, 1812
Lithograph by Weingarten

Peter Sailly wrote Macdonough on April 6 that the British fleet would probably sail to Otter Creek. They would block Macdonough's ships at the mouth of the river or sail upstream to destroy them. Macdonough immediately had batteries erected on the lake shore. On May 14 British vessels arrived at the mouth of Otter Creek. Macdonough was prepared. Soldiers from Burlington exchanged fire with the British for nearly two hours before the enemy sailed away. There were no casualties.

At the end of May Macdonough proudly sailed his fleet into Plattsburgh Bay. From his flagship, the 26-gun *Saratoga*, he wrote Mr. Jones that his "squadron was brought to an anchor...ready for service."[39] By August Macdonough had news that the British fleet on the Richelieu River at Isle aux Noix would soon meet his vessels at Plattsburgh.

Macdonough carefully and wisely planned his tactics and strategy for the battle. On September 1, 1814, he lined up his vessels in Plattsburgh Bay. It was advantageous for Macdonough to meet the enemy in a bay rather than on the broad lake, because he had short-range guns (carronades). The east side of the bay is bordered by a narrow strip of land that stretches south about two and a half miles into the lake. This point of land was known as Cumberland Head. Macdonough hoped that a north wind would make it difficult for Capt. George Downie's vessels to tack north into the bay.

Each (American) vessel was provided with springs, or hawsers, attached to the bow anchor or its cable and extended along the length of the vessel to the stern. By hauling on the port or starboard spring, the vessel could be canted (turned) one way or the other. Stern anchors were also provided in case of emergency. As a further precaution, a kedge anchor was planted broad off each bow of the *Saratoga* with a hawser leading from each quarter to the kedge on that side. Thus the control of the direction of broadsides, the possibility of a shift of wind, and the means of winding ship, if necessary, were all provided for. As it turned out, these very precautions saved the day.[40]

Macdonough anchored his squadron in a line northeast to southwest opposite Plattsburgh. The *Eagle* was at the north end, then Macdonough's flagship *Saratoga*; next the *Ticonderoga* and last the *Preble*. The *Preble* at the south end was a short distance from Crab Island. On this little island soldiers had put up tents to shelter sick and wounded men. Gunboats were located west of the vessels.

While Macdonough prepared to meet the British fleet, General Alexander Macomb prepared his small army to defend Plattsburgh from the British army. Macomb had graduated with West Point Military Academy's first class of army officers. Macomb and Macdonough were good friends and both young. They worked well together planning their tactics and strategy for a joint defense of Lake Champlain and the village of Plattsburgh.

Meanwhile General Sir George Prevost in command of the British troops and Captain George Downie of the British navy corresponded about their joint efforts to defeat the Americans. Prevost planned to capture Plattsburgh while Downie defeated Macdonough's navy.

45

On September 3, 1814, Henry Averill, age 16, was sitting at his school desk beside an open window at Plattsburgh Academy. The school was located on the lot now occupied by the Plattsburgh Public Library. When he heard the men outside say that British troops were marching toward Plattsburgh, he immediately sprang out the window without the permission of his teacher.[41] Henry joined a company of volunteer riflemen and marched north to meet the enemy. He was soon joined by sixteen classmates. Martin Aiken was chosen as their leader.

On September 6, 1814, General Prevost invaded Plattsburgh with a large well-trained army. Macomb's small force fought bravely, but they could not prevent the enemy's occupation of everything north of the Saranac River.

While Macomb's soldiers fought to protect the forts and buildings on the south side of the Saranac River, terrified citizens fled to escape the enemy. Peter Sailly wrote that "families with their goods packed in carts streamed over the bridges."[42] Again they drove through the forest to Peru. The refugees lived for nearly a week with Quaker farmers. *(The author of this story is a descendant of those Peru pioneers.)*

After the exodus from Plattsburgh, Macomb's soldiers tore up the plank flooring of bridges to prevent the British from crossing the Saranac to destroy our forts. On United States Avenue, near Plattsburgh's old cemetery, a state marker indicates the site where Fort Brown was built.

At the bridge on Bridge Street Macomb's men exchanged fire with the British on the northwest bank of the Saranac River. From the protection of a stone sawmill the teenagers of Aiken's Volunteers added their fire to the crossfire of the two armies. When Macomb dismissed Henry Averill and his classmates, he promised to give each boy a rifle. Twelve years later, each young man received from Congress a rifle with his name on it.

About nine o'clock Sunday morning September 11, 1814, Captain George Downie brought the British fleet up Lake Champlain and around Cumberland Head into Plattsburgh Bay. Because his ships had to tack into the north wind, Downie had trouble lining up his vessels between Macdonough's ships and Cumberland Head. The British vessels, *Confiance*, *Linnet*, *Chub* and *Finch* were in a trap, just as Macdonough had planned.

Crowds of people on Cumberland Head silently watched as the British ships, one by one, their ensigns fluttering in the breeze, took their place opposite the American vessels. Rodney Macdonough wrote this description of the scene on his grandfather's ship minutes before the battle commenced:

> There was now a hushed, expectant moment like the stillness which precedes the storm. Macdonough, whose manly courage was supported by a childlike faith, knelt on the deck of the flagship with his officers around him and repeated the prayer appointed by the church to be said before a fight at sea.[43]

Mueller refers to this prayer in his book. "... stir up Thy strength, O Lord, and come and help us, for Thou givest not always the battle to the strong, but canst save many or few ... through Jesus Christ, our Lord."[44]

47

Printed earthenware commemorative plate
of Commodore's victory
Historical Society of Delaware

When the British flagship *Confiance* was within range, Macdonough fired one of his long 24's. The shot killed and wounded several men. As the *Linnet* passed the *Saratoga*, she fired at the flagship and broke a cage containing a gamecock. The rooster flew into the ship's rigging, flapped his wings and crowed loudly and defiantly. The men saw this as a good omen and cheered.

As soon as Downie anchored his ship opposite the *Saratoga*, he poured his fire into Macdonough's ship. The dead and wounded were carried below. Soon after this, Captain Downie was killed by fire from the *Saratoga*.

At 10:30 Lt. Henley of the brig *Eagle* changed his position in order to fire on the *Confiance*. But he exposed the *Saratoga* to fire from the *Linnet*. Henley's maneuver put the *Saratoga* in a dangerous position. He was later reprimanded by Macdonough.

Meanwhile Macdonough was working along with his sailors. He was knocked down twice, once remaining senseless for a few minutes. A shot cut off the head of the captain of the gun and drove it against Macdonough with such force that he was knocked across the deck and fell, almost senseless, between two guns. Twice the *Confiance*'s hot shot set the *Saratoga* on fire.

When the *Saratoga*'s starboard guns no longer worked, his men were able to turn the vessel around. With cables, springs (hawsers) and anchors the ship was turned so the unused portside faced the enemy. The crew of the *Confiance* tried the same maneuver, but failed to turn the ship.

Artist's conception of the Battle of Plattsburgh

At 11:20 the British ships struck their colors. As the enemy's flags came down, shouts of joy rose from the throngs on the shore. Julius Hubbell, a young lawyer from nearby Chazy, was among the spectators and wrote this description:

> The firing was terrific, fairly shaking the ground, and so rapid that it seemed to be one continuous roar, intermingled with the spiteful flashing from the mouths of the guns, and dense clouds of smoke soon hung over the two fleets.... I saw two midshipmen go out in their small boat ... in order to swing the *Saratoga* around so as to bring her fresh broadside to bear upon her enemy, the *Confiance*.[45]

Hubbell got a canoe and boarded the *Saratoga*. He shook hands with Macdonough and congratulated him. The dead were all packed up in order here, and the decks were cleaned up, but the seams were full of blood, ... the torn hull, masts and spars told the story of the fearful struggle. He went on the *Confiance* where the decks were strewed with mutilated bodies lying in all directions, and everything was covered with blood.

When Macdonough heard the shouts of joy from the shore and saw the British flags come down, he must have reverently thanked Almighty God for His help in defeating the British navy. Macdonough's report to Secretary of the Navy Jones described the conquered squadron:

> I could only look at the enemy's galleys going off in a shattered condition; for there was not a mast in

either squadron that could stand to make sail on; the lower rigging, being nearly all shot away, hung down as though it had just been placed over the mast heads.[46]

The Americans lost 4 officers and 48 men and 58 wounded. The British lost 5 officers and 49 men and 116 wounded.[47]

It is obvious that Macdonough's foresight, valor, ingenuity and perseverance won the day. It is not generally known that he was a kind and thoughtful young officer. When the British officers came to the *Saratoga* for the formal surrender, they offered their swords to Macdonough. He politely told the men to keep their swords because they were "worthy of them." Then he ordered an officer to take the prisoners to nearby Crab Island, to "treat them kindly and speak to them encouragingly."[48] The wounded were taken to the hospital on the island. The dead of Britain and America were buried in a common grave south of the hospital tents on the north end of the island. A monument in their memory stands there today.

A half hour after the victory, a gig from the *Saratoga* rowed to Plattsburgh with the following dispatch to Secretary Jones in Washington:

> *U.S. Ship Saratoga* off Plattsburgh
> September 11, 1814
> Sir; The Almighty has been pleased to grant us a signal victory on Lake Champlain in the capture of one frigate, one brig and two sloops of war of the enemy.

I have the honor to be, very respectfully, sir, your obt (obedient) servt (servant).

T,Macdonough Com'g[49]

On September 13 Macdonough wrote Secretary Jones another letter. Because his health had not been good during the months of harsh winter weather, Macdonough asked for a new assignment in a mild climate. His request was denied.

Three days after the battle a burial service was held for British and American officers. They were buried with honors in the village cemetery. Most of the inscriptions on the grave stones are still legible.

Macdonough received many letters of congratulation. On September 19 Secretary of the Navy Jones wrote: "It is not alone the brilliancy of your victory in a naval view, but its importance and beneficial results that will fix the attention and command the gratitude of your admiring country."[50]

Macdonough's close friend, Captain William Bainbridge, wrote:

Your victory on Champlain will be a bright ornament in our naval history, and your name, my friend, will descend to our children with admiration for the hero of that lake. . . May you long live for your country's sake is the prayer of your sincere friend,

Wm. Bainbridge[51]

When the firing ceased on the lake, a messenger on horseback raced to Plattsburgh to give the good news to Macomb's army and the citizens still in the village. His men had fought valiantly to stop the British from crossing the Saranac River. By evening the enemy had commenced a hasty retreat to Canada.

Plattsburgh families soon returned to a battered village. "From September 6 until evening of the 11th, scarcely a building escaped injury ... nine houses, thirteen stores, the courthouse and jail were burned."[52]

When Henry and Betsey Delord and their baby daughter returned to Plattsburgh, they found their store and property severely damaged. The British officers who had occupied their house for five days left the rooms in great disorder. In their hasty retreat, the officers left a tea chest. There it remains today at the old Kent-Delord House Museum. We can picture the Delords rushing to their garden, digging up their silver set, and expressing the wish they would never again bury their silver.

Following the victory there was great rejoicing and gratitude for the skill and courage of the navy and army. According to Plattsburgh's weekly newspaper, the *Republican*, the citizens decided "to give Commodore Macdonough a public dinner in honor and celebration of the important victory obtained by him on the 11th."[53] They appointed Peter Sailly president of the committee and Henry Delord chairman of arrangements.

On September 20 Henry Delord with his committee called on Commodore Macdonough on board the *Saratoga*. They presented him with Henry's written invitation to the dinner September 23 at Israel Green's Hotel

City Park
Vergennes, Vermont

on Bridge Street. In his note of acceptance, Macdonough politely and firmly stated he would bring with him "six or seven"[54] officers of his squadron. He was kind to his officers and thought they deserved to be invited. Of course Henry quickly assured his friend that the committee would be pleased to invite his officers.

The Plattsburgh newspaper published a detailed account of the celebration at the hotel. From three o'clock until evening citizens and officers had a jolly time. They enjoyed the excellent dinner provided by Mr. Green. General Macomb entertained them with his "fine band of musick." The guests were honored with appropriate toasts of praise and gratitude. Macdonough referred to Captain Downie as "our brave enemy." One of the speakers offered a toast to the hero of the battle: "May he not be forgotten by his country."[55]

Plattsburgh's celebration was the first of many tributes that Macdonough received. His country promoted him to the rank of captain as of September 11, 1814. The State of New York gave him 2000 acres of land in Cayuga County. Vermont purchased a farm of 200 acres on the west side of Cumberland Head as a gift to the young captain. In the summer his descendants occupy a cottage on the Macdonough farm. It overlooks the scene of their ancestor's triumph. Macdonough's native state of Delaware gave him a sword, a silver tea set and had his portrait painted.

The whole country praised Macdonough's victory as equal to Commodore Perry's on Lake Erie September 10, 1813. The Battle of Plattsburgh is one of the decisive battles in American history. It prevented the invasion and conquest of New York State as effectively in 1814 as the surrender of the British under Burgoyne did in 1777.[56]

Captain Thomas Macdonough was thirty years old when he won the laurels he deserved. For two years he conquered every possible obstacle to build a fleet that would defeat the enemy. Although he was a strict commander, he was concerned with the welfare of his officers and men. He was courteous to the British officers and kind to his prisoners. Only a deeply religious young lieutenant would kneel in prayer on his ship's deck before a battle.

Chapter IV
The Last Command

On October 2, 1814, Thomas Macdonough said good-bye to Plattsburgh. He then took the fleet up the lake to put it in winter quarters at Whitehall. At the south end of the lake the ships were the greatest distance from a possible British attack.

On November 12, Captain Macdonough formally turned the squadron over to Lt. Charles Budd. The hero's duty on Lake Champlain had come to a victorious conclusion. With "every possible exertion,"[57] with foresight, perseverance and skill Thomas Macdonough fulfilled his orders to command the navy on the lake.

On the tenth of December Macdonough arrived in Middletown. There was great joy in the family when he gathered Lucy Ann and their little son in his arms.

Not to be outdone by banquets at Burlington, Albany and Troy, Middletown, Connecticut, honored its adopted son with a dinner and ball at the Washington Hotel December 21. The *Middletown Spectator* said:

> The ball has never been equalled in this place. . .
> The presence of Commodore Macdonough and his
> lady produced universal satisfaction . . . friends and
> townsmen gave a tribute of affection to their modest, estimable fellow citizen and their homage of
> respect to the illustrious defender of his country.[58]

Lucy Ann and her family were concerned about Macdonough's health. He looked very tired and thin.

The last of December Captain Macdonough was ordered to New York to command the steam war frigate, *Fulton The First*. He was the first commander of the first steam war vessel in the world.[59]

On January 6, New York City welcomed Macdonough and presented him with a certificate of freedom of the city in a gold box. At a later date the city paid John Wesley Jarvis $400 to paint a full length portrait of Macdonough.[60] In the large painting the captain looks handsome in his full dress uniform. He has blue eyes, curly hair and a firm mouth and chin. Battleships of Plattsburgh can be seen in the background. Macdonough's portrait was hung beside the portrait of General Alexander Macomb in City Hall in New York.

In January the governor of New York was apprehensive that the British would return and attack the vessels at Whitehall. On the 7th Macdonough was ordered to Whitehall. After checking with Lt. Budd on the security of the squadron, he went to Burlington and from there to Plattsburgh.

He was probably a house guest of the Delords when he wrote the Secretary of the Navy the first of February 1815. Macdonough said the vessels at Whitehall were safe for the present. He added that the British were building a new fleet at Isle aux Noix for a possible appearance on the lake in September. He listed the names of capable officers for the command and concluded his letter with a request that he "not be placed again in command on the lake."[61]

On February 3 he returned to Whitehall where he remained until the Senate on February 17, 1815, ratified the peace treaty signed at Ghent December 24, 1814. The War of 1812 was the last contest between English-speaking nations.

Following a business trip to Washington in May, 1815, Macdonough enjoyed a visit with his brothers and sisters, friends and neighbors at the Trap. The State of Delaware paid tribute to their illustrious native son and arranged with the artist, Thomas Sully, to paint his portrait. The painting hangs in the House Chamber in the Old State House in Dover.

In 1816 Macdonough returned to Plattsburgh to confer with a committee selecting a site for fortifications at the village. No doubt he stayed at the Delord home.

The state of New York in 1817 invited Macdonough to Albany for the presentation of a sword. Since the February weather was extremely cold and Macdonough was not well, Governor Thompkins went to Hartford, Connecticut, to meet Macdonough. Again the hero was honored with a banquet, music, patriotic songs and toasts.

The following year the Navy Department ordered Macdonough to take command of the frigate *Guerriere*. In July, 1818, the frigate left Boston to take George Campbell, U.S. minister, to Russia. After leaving the Campbells at St. Petersburg in October, Macdonough's ship cruised in the Mediterranean. At Naples he was presented to the Emperor of Austria and the King of Naples.

Macdonough returned to the United States in 1820. In March he was ordered to command the ship *Ohio 74* then under construction. She was launched May 30.

For the next four years Macdonough spent much of his time at home. Lucy Ann was not well and she was glad for his help. They had ten children, but five died young. The children who survived were James, Charles Shaler, Augustus Rodney, Thomas and Charlotte.

During the autumn of 1822 Macdonough made his last journey to visit Plattsburgh and the Delords. In October of that year Henry Delord wrote in his diary:

> We have had a visit of Commodore Macdonough in the beginning of October. . . . A committee was appointed to invite him to a public dinner which he declined. . . . I think he was partial of his time with my family.[62]

It may have been during this visit that Macdonough gave the Delords his picture to show his appreciation of their friendship and hospitality. The little portrait was done by George Freeman, a self-taught folk artist who painted miniature portraits for about ten dollars.[63] In the water-color picture Macdonough wore his full dress uniform with both epaulets. On the left epaulet the artist signed his name: "G. Freeman, painter." Henry and Betsey were delighted to have the little portrait. They were not surprised that the young officer in the miniature looked tired. This portrait still hangs on the wall in the east parlor of the Kent-Delord House Museum.

On October 20, 1824, Captain Thomas Macdonough, commanding the frigate *Constitution*, set sail for the Mediterranean to take charge of the United States naval force.

61

Freeman Portrait of Macdonough

During their twelve years of marriage Thomas and Lucy Ann said goodby many times. Their farewell this time was sadly different. Lucy Ann's health was fast failing. The previous year she wrote a friend, Abby Chew, that she must find all possible means "for lengthening a life which I have for many months known could not continue long."[64]

On the Mediterranean assignment Macdonough took his four-year-old son, Augustus Rodney Macdonough, named for Caesar Augustus Rodney of Delaware. We wonder why Macdonough took his little son away from his family on such a long voyage. Perhaps Rodney's absence from home left one less child for Lucy Ann's family to care for. It is almost certain that Rodney, fascinated by his father's stories of exciting adventures at sea, begged Macdonough to take him on the cruise.

In the fall of 1825 the news of Lucy Ann's death, August 9, reached Macdonough in the Mediterranean. He was now desperately ill with tuberculosis, weighing only sixty pounds,[65] so that this message devastated him. Lucy Ann was thirty-five years old. It was not easy for Macdonough to tell little Rodney his mother was dead. It must have been additionally difficult to explain to him that his father himself was so ill that they must sail for home.

When Macdonough was carried from the *Constitution* to the merchant ship *Edwin*, Rodney and the ship's doctor, William Turk, were with him. Captain Thomas Macdonough died on the *Edwin* November 10, 1825, six hundred miles from the country he fought to save. On his last command Macdonough was only forty-one years old.

After the *Edwin* arrived at Philadelphia, Dr. Turk wrote to Lucy Ann's mother, Mrs. Shaler. He described

Macdonough's last days and his wish to be taken home for interment. He did not want to be "thrown into the sea"[66] as was the custom at that time for death on a ship. He said little Rodney was with him and in good health.

Dr. Turk and officials arrived at New York with Macdonough's body the 27th of November. At the Battery Dr. Turk handed his little charge over to Rodney's uncle, the Rev. Mr. Rutledge. They then joined a procession of officers of the army and navy, pall bearers with the coffin, the Society of the Cincinnati, clergy, citizens, and a marine band with muffled drums. The body was carried to the common council chamber at City Hall for military honors. The procession was re-formed and walked to St. Paul's Chapel. At the conclusion of the service at St. Paul's, the march was continued to the Fulton Street dock.

Here the coffin was placed on board a steamship to be taken to Middletown, Connecticut. Dr. Turk and Rev. Rutledge were on board with the commodore's son. Rodney must have been a tired little boy. He was probably glad to leave New York with its mournful sound of tolling church bells and the funereal march music of marine bands.

The ship arrived at Middletown Saturday morning, December 3. At one o'clock the coffin was taken to the Presbyterian Church for an Episcopal service.

Thomas Macdonough was buried with military, civil and Masonic honors beside his beloved Lucy Ann Shaler Macdonough at Riverside Cemetery. The following inscriptions are on the single monument that marks their graves:

Sacred
to the memory of
Com. Thomas Macdonough
of the U.S. Navy.
He was born in the State of Delaware Dec. 1783, & died at sea of
pulmonary consumption while
on his return from the command
of the American Squadron in the
Mediterranean on the 10 Nov. 1825.
He was distinguished in the world
as the Hero of Lake Champlain; in
the Church of Christ as a faithful, zealous
and consistent Christian; in the com-
munity where he resided when absent
from professional duties as an amiable,
upright and valuable citizen.

Sacred
to the memory of
Mrs. Lucy Ann,
Wife of
Com. Thomas Macdonough
& daughter of
Nathaniel & Lucy Ann Shaler.
The richest gifts of Nature & of Grace
adorned her mind and heart, & at her
death Genius, Friendship and Piety
mourned their common loss.
She preceded her husband to the realms
of Glory only a few short months, having
departed this life Aug. 9, 1825, AE. 35.

They were lovely and pleasant in their lives,
and in their death they were undivided.[67]

Six miles south of Middletown, Delaware, nearby the old McDonough homestead, an old, low brick wall protects the little family cemetery. Inscriptions on eight weather-worn gravestones give only the name, date of death and age of James McDonough and his family. From these patriotic Delaware ancestors Captain Thomas Macdonough inherited the skills and determination that helped our country again win her freedom from Great Britain.

At Plattsburgh, New York, a large bronze eagle on a tall commemorative monument keeps watch over the site of Thomas Macdonough's victory on Lake Champlain.

Macdonough family home, 1990

Chapter V
Old Paths Anew

Deborah P. Haskell, Ph.D.

Historical records even in the *Small Wonder State* of Delaware don't always contain all the details necessary to complete a story. Over the last several years, several researchers at the Delaware Heritage Commission, seeking more information about the life of Captain Thomas Macdonough, Delaware born hero of the War of 1812, dug deep and long but somehow the best remembrances in both Delaware and the state of New York, where his most famous Battle of Lake Champlain occurred, only begin when the young seaman reached the age of sixteen.

This digging took a number of directions. First, all the primary source materials were searched, but there were few and those discovered contained little more about Thomas. Primary source materials are things like deeds to the land, court records, letters written from one member of the family to another—in other words original documents from which researchers can piece together a story of the lives of the family. Discovered were several new letters written from Caesar A. Rodney about the captain. Although various records refer to a journal that the captain wrote while he was at sea, that is missing. The Historical Society of Delaware has in its archives the original ship's log from the *U. S. Frigate Constellation of 44 Guns 1802-1803* written by Thomas Macdonough under the captaincy of Alex Murray. The log is faded and at times is difficult to read. It describes in good form the longitude, latitude, and

69

depth of the waters, the strength of the wind and the activity of the crew during the course of each day. Some days are more hectic than others. The first page describes the ship's departure from Cape Henlopen and Delaware. It was on its way to the Mediterranean. It reads:

Monday, 15th March 1802
Light breeses and pleasant weather.
At 2 p.m. discharged the Pilot.
At 3 abreast Cape Henlopen.
At 5 p.m. Cape Henlopen bears N.W.B.W. Distant
   5 Leagues. Took our departure.
Midnight Moderate breeses and clear weather.
At 6 a.m. saw 2 sail standing to the East.

Made and shortened sail occasionally.
Variation 6 degrees westerly.[68]

Virginia Burdick, the writer of this book, has used the Rodney Macdonough biography as one of her sources of information. Rodney Macdonough's book is a secondary source although he used letters and family memorabilia in its preparation. In a secondary source, the author sometimes draws conclusions which are not warranted from the primary sources. That is why a reader must feel free to accept or reject secondary sources.

From a number of primary sources, there are known facts about the family. Known are the occupations of Thomas's father and grandfather. And, knowing those indicate the kind of lifestyle to which young Thomas must have been accustomed. Both his father and grandfather

South side porch, McDonough family home 1991

were doctors. Therefore, one assumes that Thomas, Jr. was not poor, that he probably had enough to eat.

We know also that, during Thomas Jr.'s very early years, the frictions between the Whigs (Yankee Patriots for independence from the Crown) and Tories (the English who were loyal to the King of England and who wanted America to remain under British rule) were occurring. From reading the works of other historians a reader may conclude that life during those times was precarious. It must have been like living among spies—you didn't always know whether your neighbor's allegiances were to the English Crown or to an independent America. In a book about the ancestry of the McDonoughs, there are several letters written from a young soldier who was assigned to Major Thomas McDonough's regiment near Lewes, Delaware (then spelled Lewis). The captain's father, the major, was in charge of a detachment of about two hundred men in May and June 1776, the purpose of which was to prevent an uprising among the Tories of Sussex County. The quotation which follows is from that soldier named Enoch Anderson. Through this letter, the reader will see and feel that this geographical area was in a turmoil and that the times were desperate. There seemed to be very few Whigs compared with Tories. In more normal non-war time, an older man would have been given the following duties if there had been any men to spare. These words of Enoch tell how he became an adjutant general.

All was alarm at our garrison: the Whig militia and many officers had come in and put themselves under the protection of our little army, and to give what aid they could, but our whole force did not amount to more than three hundred men. We had one "long Tom" (probably a gun) . . . the alarm increased. I think it was the third day after my arrival that we were surrounded by about fifteen hundred Tories.... The Major came to me and took me . . . to General Dagworthy. "This," says our Major, "is the young man I have recommended to your notice." "Why," says the General, "this is but a beardless boy." "No matter," said the Major, "I think him fitted to the office you may appoint him." The General said, "You must be well informed of our dangerous situation. Here are five British men-of-war in the Bay right opposite us . . . we, therefore, young man do constitute and appoint you Adjutant General *pro tem*, under the command of the Major McDonough. The Tories (said he) are mostly armed with guns, and those that have not guns have pitchforks and... clubs. . . . Be careful—be vigilant . . .[69]

So, life was pretty tense just fifty miles away from young Thomas. Life must also have been very harrowing for the major's brother, Micah, who was in the state of Ohio battling the American Indians. Although the subjugation of the native peoples of America is now a sad commentary in American political history, it is nonetheless a reality of the times. Micah was probably James's youngest son. Records state that he became an ensign in the 2nd infantry on March 4, 1791. He was promoted to lieutenant on March 5, 1792, and then to the 2nd sublegion on September 4, 1792, eventually dismissed on December 29, 1793.[70]

73

A letter discovered in the Historical Society of Delaware Library was written from Micah to his brother Patrick and contains a record of the battles Micah's company was engaged in from August 12, 1791, when they arrived in Ohio, until the date of the letter November 10, 1791, as part of the expansion of the American west. It is written from the perspective of a white American engaged in a war with his enemy, the American Indian. It indicates prejudice toward the Indians who seemed to have the upper hand in these battles. But in a positive vein, the letter also gives a flavor of the family style—some humor and some irreverence. We shall quote from the beginning of this letter, the middle, and the end. Needless to say, Micah was a lucky survivor.

Dear Patt.
Be assured, its a pleasure for me to embrace an opportunity of informing you that I am Alive, and well, altho such a great numbers of my acquaintances and friends have lately changed their place of abode, and that without the hair of their heads. The American Arms never met with such a defeat
. . . .
. . . proceed on the fourth of October, Our Army consisting of about eighteen hundred effectives, infantry—one hundred and fifty artillery and eighty light dragoons—Our movements were very slow and attended with the greatest fatigue imaginable, in cutting a road through such a wilderness—we halted forty four miles from Fort Hamilton (delightful country) and erected a well constructed strong

74

Grave of Dr. Thomas McDonough,
father of the captain

garrison called Fort Jefferson—During which time we almost starved to death, The duty being severe and on half allowance, from Fort Jefferson, we proceeded on with a fresh supply of provision, slowly, through a low swampy (tho fertile) countryside scarcely passable, Thirty three miles to the place of action which happened on the fourth of this inst: . . .the third of November We encamp, on a rising piece of ground on some of the Wabash waters, surrounded with lone swampy land, full of underbrush and old logs, which answered their purpose very well, during the night they keep us awake by their constant stir around our camp. . . .

We left every thing behind, eight pieces of cannon, cattle, horses, flour, officers and soldiers, baggage, officers, private property in cash, supposed to be ten thousand pounds, besides all their clothing, We retreated, day and night for this place, without provision, which is ninety eight miles and arrived at this place on the eight inst: Inclosed is a list of the many brave officers that fell—the number of noncommissioned officers, music and privates that fell in the field, is upwards of six hundred, sixty odd women were killed. . . .

My God, I shall say no more about it, only add that as there were such havock made in our regiment, I shall in the couple or six or eight months, write captain after my name and that I am your

affectionate brother
Micah McDonough
2nd U. S. Regiment[71]

The Heritage Commission researchers wanted desperately to tell you readers about how young Thomas spent his time growing up but cannot except by conjecture from the few primary sources already mentioned. If Major McDonough was fifty miles away defending America from the British, chances are Thomas was left to his own devices perhaps to wait for war news and pretend as people do now with war games.

The number of brothers and sisters Thomas had is known. The captain's brothers were James, Samuel, John and Joseph. His sisters were Hannah, Mary, Hester and Lydia. Brother James was older and was in the Navy before Thomas was grown. Grandfather James was still living and, although his eyesight was very poor, he may have been surrogate father while Dad was off fighting. Also fighting were brother James and Uncle Micah and perhaps other family members. Grandfather James died at the age of 80 in January of 1792. He outlived his wife Lydia, and a daughter Bridget, who died in 1773. Studying the gravestones in the McDonough family cemetery, with the help of a little mathematical calculation, allows for this conclusion. Other families whom the individual McDonoughs married were Roberts, Vance, Hubbard, Hart and McNunn.

Walking around in the house in which young Thomas grew up provides some clues to his illusive life. Visible in the main room is the place where the stairway to the upstairs bedrooms was originally located. The visitor can see and imagine fires in the winter in the large fireplace in the large front room where the family gathered. You also can stand in the very room that young Thomas thought up pranks like any other young person, look out the windows over the fields as Thomas did, although there are more houses on the horizon now than there were in his time. Notice how flat the land is and how green the grass. Imagine him watching sunsets and rain storms and figure that he had some dreams of going to sea like his brother James. Old photographs of the family home show large trees in the front yard that are not there any more. The proportions look different due to the fact that present day photographic equipment is better and current photographs are more true to the size and shape of the objects.

Known also is what the weather was like in Delaware in the late eighteenth century. Although meteorologists assert that winters are getting warmer and the coastline is eroding a bit along the beach resorts, Delaware does occupy a temperate climate. By comparison, the weather was much colder in New York State where Thomas and Lucy lived during the preparation for the battle of Lake Champlain. Known are some of the foods Thomas enjoyed. The reader may find this a little unsettling, but read on. In a letter to a friend, Commodore Chew, written from Middletown, Connecticut, Thomas discusses their food preferences.

Dear Sir:
I send per sloop Robert McCleave a half barrel of shad and a small box from Mrs. M. of southern hommany. . . . The shad is high, $6.25 though I suspect it is good. I spoke for 1 1/2 barrels for myself, but could obtain but one. I suppose you know you must keep a small board with stone on it in the barrel, to keep the fish under the brine. And

78

Current homestead and barns

when you take a piece for use, endeavor to do it without permitting it to touch the stuff or scum that floats on the top—by pulling it outside by hand. The fish are better the second year; we are now using those of 3 years and we think them even better.[72]

Have you eaten shad? In brine and/or three years old? Do you like hominy?

Thomas went to school, and it is rumored that there was a school right across the road from his home. He was not pampered, in terms of education. In some well-to-do homes, a tutor was brought in to teach the children. Not so with Thomas. He went to a "country school," which means he went out of the home to school, like you do. He was a pretty good speller. That can be deduced from reading his letters, although he used very long sentences and he sometimes forgot to start a new sentence with a capital letter. Other writers, like Micah, put in too many capital letters and no periods at ends of sentences.

Thomas's personality (modest, thoughtful, and with a sense of humor) can be surmised from a number of documents. Among these are a letter that Thomas himself wrote to the navy and letters which people from the Lake Champlain battle wrote about him. The General Assembly of Delaware asked Nicholas Ridgely to write about his friend Thomas. He says almost those same words.

The commodore, after his father's death, obtained midshipman's warrant. I used my endeavour to provide him this warrant. From this period until his return to Delaware last summer I never saw him.

80

He appears to be extremely modest and reserved. In June or July last I was frequently in company with him. I never heard him speak a word of his exploits. On one or two occasions I endeavored to lead the conversation to his services and the Battle on the Lake but could never press (anything out of him).

. . . .

I have heard that the commodore was very kind to his relations when on a visit to them last Spring and Winter I found among those who had been intimate with him last summer that he has the reputation of being a very religious man. This is a noble trait in his character.[73]

Caesar A. Rodney emphasized in a separate letter that the captain was "perfectly free from vanity and pride. His glorious affair on Champlain has not produced the slightest change in his character."[74]

Not only do the men of his time stipulate that Thomas was a good person but, from a thank you note that he sent back to Caesar Augustus Rodney, the reader finds a humble man. The continuing thanks he expresses over and over again and the modesty he shows as appreciation for every little honor bestowed on him seems to prove the flattering comments made about him. This letter also exhibits a little humor when he describes in a very characteristic way the battle on Lake Champlain as though he were not in a real way responsible for the success of that event.

Dear Sir:

In consequence of my long stay on Lake Champlain after my return thither in January last, I did not receive your letter until yesterday, as I expected to return to my home every day and the Post Dispatcher did not forward it to me. I now take the earliest opportunity to express to you my thanks for the very friendly and handsome interest you have taken for me in the Legislature of my native state. The resolution of which honorable body in voting me the sword and service of state is very flattering and truly satisfactory. I hope my future life will merit this notice taken of me. The other part of the resolutions that of sitting for my portrait is also highly flattering to me and shall be cheerfully complied with. Since my good fortune in the service I have more than every great cause to thank you for the service you did me in attaining me my warrant as a midshipman in the navy. You were the means of my continuance in it also under that establishment and it was very gratifying to me to receive your congratulatory letter of the 20th September 1814 soon after we had what old seamen called a very desperate engagement. I propose visiting Washington in a few days and afterwards to stay some time among our friends in Delaware where I hope to have the pleasure to seeing yourself.

I am with much respect and esteem your obedient servant.   T. Macdonough[75]

Rodney and Louise McDonough at ancestral cemetery
1990

It is difficult to understand how a person who had tuberculosis for ten years and yellow fever when he was sixteen could be as cheerful as he was in this letter.

What was Thomas's dear wife Lucy like? In addition to the winters being very cold in New York State and there being little heat in the house, add to these the difficulties of having children without the benefit of modern medicine. It was a difficult time.

Nonetheless, Lucy was a gentle woman with a good perspective on life, trying not to complain of her lot too much. The following excerpts provide glimpses of her life as a navy wife. She writes her mother from Vermont, exhibiting a similar quiet humor to Thomas's, employing words like "pericranium" to poke fun at herself.

Dear Mother . . . I do not know how people can live without some particular object or pursuit. It appears to me that an idle life or one not employed to some end . . . is a perfect misery. . . . I am confident we lose our facilities by not keeping them in use, and I am sure the last fifteen months have reduced my ideas to a thimbleful, and unless these form a contract and, as Godwin would say, "generate" new ones, I shall have my pericranium left void. I read till I get dizzy and sleepy, then I sew a little, then I knit; but even sewing, reading, and knitting do not fill up the vacuum. The good woman with whom I live takes every pains to make me comfortable. I worked up a cap for her sister and she sent me a pie. The people here are very clever but it is not a season when they can be very sociable, as you are liable to

drown in the mud. I await the weather to settle to
ride on horse back. I have the offer of as many
horses as I can ride.[76]

At one point she writes her mother that they are being
evicted from the house they are living in. She says,

> The lady who charitably took us to board has con-
> cluded she can keep us no longer. Accordingly we
> depart bag and baggage on Tuesday. Like the
> shilling who said he went through so many hands,
> our "next owner" is Col. Fisher. . . . There is a
> universal dread of officers among the enlightened
> inhabitants. . . .
>
> I hope you will think seriously about coming up
> for me. It will be a pleasant jaunt for you by the
> middle of June. . . .[77]

And people in those days lived with a lot more death and
dying. The captain's wife died about the same time he did.
He lost a number of progeny before any lived long enough
to run around and play like normal children. (Five of his
ten children died young.) A letter to his sister Lydia in
Delaware talks of this. And this was written after the battle
success of Lake Champlain. A person could not be too self-
satisfied in light of the human tragedy occurring in domes-
tic life all around him or her. He says:

> It will grieve you, my dear sister, to hear that
> yesterday I buried my other son. Poor dear boy, he
> was but 12 hours sick with an inflammation in the

Richard Rodney Willhardt at family cemetery 1989

lungs and cutting teeth at the same time. . . two sweet boys have I now lost in less than two years...[78]

A later letter to Lydia is more optimistic. Here we see a father's pride with some of the usual good humor.

My own children are James Edward, Charles Shaler, Augustus Rodney–and Thomas. So you see I have four boys and I am sure, setting aside the common partialities of a father, they are smart, intelligent, well-behaved children.... I wish to give ... my own children as good an education as I am able to ... and then they must shift for themselves, as I did through a dangerous and laborious minority apprenticeship of 13 years . . .[79]

Since 1989 the State of Delaware has declared September 11, the date of the victory on Lake Champlain, Commodore Thomas McDonough Day in Delaware with a celebration taking place at a school named for him in St. Georges, Delaware, about three miles north of the homestead. Governor Michael N. Castle was present at the first ceremony to read a proclamation prepared by the state to honor this occasion.

That same year the Delaware Congressman, Thomas R. Carper, dressed as the Commodore and taught a lesson to the children of the school during the early-morning assembly. Present at that event were Richard Rodney Willhardt from Colorado, a great-great-great-grandson of the captain. In one of these photos, Rod is sharing a joke with the two Delaware public servants. In another of these

Congressman Thomas R. Carper impersonating the
Commodore, descendant Richard Rodney Willhardt,
and Delaware's Governor Michael N. Castle, 1989

photographs, Rodney is investigating the graves in the family cemetery. He is battling the overgrown grasses, and searching for the grave of his ancestor.

In 1990, Rodney McDonough and his wife, Louise, came by invitation to Delaware to join in the second annual Thomas McDonough Day on September 11. Rodney is the grandfather of Rod Willhardt.

During the 1990 assembly, Chuck Eurich, a teacher from the local Gunning Bedford School, impersonated the Commodore. Malcolm Mackenzie of Wilmington described the naval battle on Lake Champlain from the point of view of the common sailor and Jean Bingham read an anonymous poem about the battle in progress. Music was provided by the middle school band.

In 1991, this book will be presented to the people of Delaware and especially to the young people who will help keep Thomas's memory alive.

Fields around the Trap

Endnotes

1. The State Constitution, framed in 1776, established an upper house called the Legislative Council and a lower house named the House of Assembly. The members were mostly farmers and land-owners with a sprinkling of lawyers, physicians and flour millers. . . . This house was a training ground for politicians who might be elected to the upper house or national office. The Legislative Council specialized in proposing amendments and revisions to bills submitted by the lower house. . . . The constitution also provided for a president (governor) as chief executive who carried on his duties with the help of a Privy Council of four members, two being elected by each house. . . . This constitution also set up a system of courts. (Harold B. Hancock, *Delaware: Two Hundred Years Ago: 1780-1800*, Middle Atlantic Press, 1987, p. 117-18.)

2. Rodney Macdonough, *Life of Commodore Thomas Macdonough, U. S. Navy*. (Boston: Fort Hill Press, 1909), p. 15.

3. Daniel R. Griffith, Nomination Form Application, National Register of Historic Places, item 8 page 1.

4. Letter, Lewis Vandegrift, memoirs, Papers on the Historical Society of Delaware XVII, 1897, p.

5. Macdonough. pp. 38-39.

6. *Ibid.*, p. 20.

7. *Ibid.*, p. 21.

8. Rodney Macdonough, Address before the Historical Society of Delaware, January 18, 1897, Papers on the Historical Society of Delaware, XVII, 1897, p. 7.

9. Macdonough, *Life,* p. 41.

10. *Ibid.,* p. 43.

11. Letter, Nicholas Ridgely to Thomas Macdonough, circa 1815, Hagley Museum and Library, Macdonough Letter file.

12. McDonough, *Life,* p. 22.

13. *Ibid.*, p. 68.

14. *Ibid.*, p. 69.

15. Frank C. Bowen, *America Sails the Seas*, (New York: Travel Publishers, Robert N. McBridge & Co., 1938), p. 169.

16. Macdonough, *Life,* p. 72.

17. *Ibid.,* p. 24.

18. Macdonough, *Address,* 1897, p. 10.

19. *Ibid.,* pp. 13-14.

20. Macdonough, *Life,* pp. 24-25.

21. *Ibid.*, p. 86.

22. Charles G. Muller, *The Proudest Day,* (New York: The John Day Company, 1960), pp. 340-341.

23. Macdonough, *Life,* pp. 91-92.

24. *Ibid.*, p. 25.

25. *Ibid.*, p. 98.

26. *Ibid.*, pp. 100-101.

27. *Ibid.*, p. 26.

28. Allan S. Everest, *The War of 1812 in the Champlain Valley,* (Syracuse, New York: Syracuse University Press, 1981), p. 64.

29. Peter S. Palmer, *Historic Sketch of Plattsburgh, New York,* (Plattsburgh: Plattsburgh Republican, 1893), pp. 27 & 33.

30. Macdonough, *Life,* p. 108.

31. *Ibid.*, p. 168.

32. Although, on the map Plattsburgh appears to be *up* the lake from Whitehall it is in fact down the lake because the water flows north.

33. Macdonough, *Life,* p. 27.

34. Muller, p. 90.

35. *Ibid.*, p. 92.

36. Macdonough, *Life,* p. 27.

37. *Ibid.*, pp. 120-121.

38. *Ibid.*, p. 144.

39. *Ibid.*, p. 147.

40. *Ibid.*, p. 172.

41. Stacey Leege, *Aiken's Volunteers,* (Plattsburgh: North Country Notes, Clinton County Historical Association, April 1980), no page number.

42. George S. Bixby, *Peter Sailly, 1754-1826,* (Albany: University of the State of New York, 1919), p. 45.

43. Macdonough, *Life,* p. 177.

44. Muller, p. 312.

45. Duane Hurd, ed. *History of Clinton and Franklin Counties, New York.* (Philadelphia: J.W. Lewis, 1880), p. 293.

46. Plattsburgh Centenary Commission, 1926, p. 42.

47. Everest, p. 185.

48. Macdonough, *Life,* p. 185.

49. *Ibid.*

50. *Ibid.*, p. 194.

51. *Ibid.*

52. Plattsburgh, New York, *Republican*, October 1, 1814, no page numbers.

53. *Ibid.*, September 24 and October 1, 1814.

54. Captain Thomas Macdonough's letter to Henry Delord, September 20, 1814. Kent-Delord Collection.

55. *Republican*, September 24 and October 1, 1814.

56. Plattsburgh Centenary Commission, p. 78.

57. Macdonough, *Life*, p. 120.

58. *Ibid.*, p. 212.

59. *Ibid.*, pp. 214-15.

60. Harold Dickson, *John Wesley Jarvis, American Painter*, 1780-1840, (New York Historical Society, 1949), p. 358.

61. Macdonough, *Life*, p. 220.

62. Henry Delord's Diary, October 1822, (State University of New York: Feinberg Library, Kent-Delord Collection).

63. Wilma Keyes, *George Freeman, Miniaturist, 1789-1868*, (Storrs: Mansfield Connecticut Historical Society, 1980), p. 15.

64. Muller, p. 330.

65. *Ibid.*

66. Macdonough, *Life,* p. 251.

67. *Ibid.,* pp. 255-56.

68. Log kept on board the *U.S. Frigate Constellation,* Alex Murray, Capt. 1802-1803. (Given to the Historical Society of Delaware by Mrs. John Elliott, Newark, Delaware, May 1891)

69. Ronald Macdonough, *McDonough-Hackstaff Ancestry,* (Boston: Press of Samuel Usher, 1901), p. 471.

70. Francis B. Heitman, *Historical Register and Dictionary of the U. S. Army, from its Organization September 29, 1789, to March 2, 1903,* Vol. 1. (Washington, D.C.: Government Printing Office, 1903).

71. Letter from Micah to Patrick Macdonough, November 10, 1791, Historical Society of Delaware, Macdonough Folder.

72. Muller, p. 351.

73. Letter, Nicholas Ridgely to Thomas Macdonough, *op. cit.*

74. Letter from Caesar Augustus Rodney, April 9, 1815, Hagley Museum and Library, McDonough Folder.

75. Letter, Thomas Macdonough to Caesar A. Rodney, April 9, 1815, Hagley Museum & Library, McDonough Folder.

76. Muller, p. 347.

77. *Ibid.* p. 348.

78. *Ibid.,* p. 349.

79. *Ibid.*, p. 352.

Bibliography

Analectic Magazine . . . Excerpts, Wilmington, Delaware, Federal Writers Project, University of Delaware, 1938.

Bixby, George S. *Peter Sailly, 1754-1826.* Albany: University of the State of New York, 1919.

Bowen, Frank C. *America Sails The Seas.* "Travel Publishers"; New York: Robert M. McBride and Co., 1938.

Burdick, Virginia M. *Love and Duty.* Plattsburgh: Kent-Delord House Museum, 1987.

Compton's Pictured Encyclopedia. *The American War of 1812.* Chicago: F. E. Compton and Company, 1954.

Dickson, Harold E. *John Wesley Jarvis American Painter 1780-1840.* New York: New York Historical Society, 1949.

Everest, Allan S. *The War of 1812 in the Champlain Valley.* Syracuse: Syracuse University Press, 1981.

Griffith, Daniel R. Nomination Form Application, National Register of Historic Places Inventory, Commodore T. Macdonough House, Hall of Records, Division of Historic and Cultural Affairs (PL89-665), May 1, 1978.

Hagley Museum and Library microfilm reproductions from the National Archives, Macdonough file.

Hancock, Harold B. *Delaware: Two Hundred Years Ago: 1780-1800*, Delaware: Middle Atlantic Press, 1987.

Heitman, Francis B. *Historical Register and Dictionary of the U.S. Army, from its organization September 29, 1789, to March 2, 1903*. (Washington, D.C.: Government Printing Office, 1903).

Historical Society of Delaware. Archives. Lewis Vandegrift Letter File, 1895.

Historical Society of Delaware, Log Kept on *U.S. Frigate Constellation*, Alex Murray, Capt. 1802-1803, (given by Mrs. John Elliott, Newark, Delaware, May 1891).

Historical Society of Delaware, Papers on the Historical Society of Delaware, XVII, 1897.

Hurd, Duane, ed. *History of Clinton and Franklin Counties, New York.* Philadelphia: J. W. Lewis, 1880.

Kent-Delord Collection. Special Collections, Feinberg Library, State University of New York, Plattsburgh.

Keyes, Wilma. *George Freeman, Miniaturist 1789-1868.* Storrs: Mansfield Connecticut Historical Society, 1980.

Leege, Stacy. *Aiken's Volunteers.* Plattsburgh: North Country Notes, Clinton County Historical Association, April 1980.

Lossing, Benson. *The Pictorial Fieldbook of the War of 1812.* New York: Harper & Brothers, 1868.

Macdonough, Rodney. *The Life of Commodore Thomas Macdonough, U. S. Navy.* Boston: Fort Hill Press, 1909.

Macdonough, Rodney. *The Macdonough-Hackstaff Ancestry.* Boston: Press of Samuel Usher, 1901.

Muller, Charles G. "Commodore and Mrs. Thomas Macdonough: Some Lights on Their Family Life," *Delaware History IX* (1960-61), pp. 341-54.

Muller, Charles G. *The Proudest Day.* New York: The John Day Company, 1960.

Palmer, Peter S. *Historical Sketch of Plattsburgh, New York.* Plattsburgh: Plattsburgh *Republican*, 1893.

Plattsburgh Centenary Commission. *The Battle of Plattsburgh.* Plattsburgh: New York State Commission, 1914.

Plattsburgh Centenary Commission. *Dedication of the Thomas Macdonough Memorial.* Plattsburgh: New York State Commission, 1926.

Plattsburgh (N.Y.) *Republican.* September 24, October 1, 1814.

Plattsburgh Sesqui-Centennial. *150th Anniversary of the Battle of Plattsburgh.* Plattsburgh: Celebration Committee, 1964.